The Moveable Feast

A picnic cookbook for all seasons

By Denise McMurry and Vicky Bittner

Introduction

Friendship is about common likeness, experiences, understanding, desires as well as shared elation, excitement, sadness, and even loneliness. Friendship stands the test of time and distance. This book is a labor of love between two friends.   Neither of us would have imagined that we would be writing a book together eight years after initially being stationed together in Germany.

Eight years that included the birth of six children, numerous moves due to our husband's jobs, and a war. This separation from our husbands only solidified our friendship. In the end, the cookbook is as much about cooking as it is about our friendship.

We found ourselves together again in Ft Hood, Texas, with both of our husbands deployed to Iraq for one year. What were we going to do to keep from going crazy-PICNICS! We did some of the most terrific day trips Texas has to offer! Our Moveable Feasts had the greatest food any five star restaurant serves.

Here we are once again, miles apart: Vicky in Colorado and Denise in the Netherlands-oh the joy of friendship.

The inspiration for this book was the fun and friendship we created with picnics while our husbands were away. Picnics do not have to take weeks of planning nor include peanut butter and jelly sandwiches. Join us on a yearlong trip into a wonderful, delicious and exciting world of picnics.   We wish you many fond memories and great food with YOUR Moveable Feast!

Enjoy all your picnics!

Vicky and Denise

Dedication

This book is for the six kids that we have so much fun with-Helena, Colin, Harrison, Ian, Graham, and Ronan. They put up with all of our crazy ideas for picnics! As well as our husbands, John and Brian-they could not share in all of our picnics, but they were always there in heart.

Acknowledgments

We are forever grateful to our family and friends for all of the pictures and constructive suggestions. Your ideas and suggestions helped put this book together! Thank You!
.

Table of Contents

We broke the book into seasons to make it easy to read and plan your picnic menu. The idea for the seasons is to take advantage of the terrific local fruits and vegetables available at each time. A picnic does not have to occur on a beautiful spring or summer day. Winter and fall have beautiful, exciting and fun advantages for picnicking as well. We hope that you will take advantage of what your area has to offer by substituting the fresh goods of your area for some of the recipes.

Ideas for Packing Food

We think the easiest way to transport your food is in re-sealable plastic bags or in lidded plastic containers. The recipe instructions are laid out to pack everything separately at home and assemble at the picnic site, but we have also found many fun and imaginative ways to carry the food. You could make individual boxes such as hat boxes, gift boxes or paper Mache boxes, paper bags decorated with stickers or Chinese take-out containers. You can wrap food in parchment paper, fun heavy-duty paper napkins or foil. You can tie the food with ribbon, twine, or strips of fabric. You can pack moist food in canning jars, re-sealable plastic bags tied with a ribbon, or fun decorated lidded containers. There are also many different kinds of picks and skewers out there for decorating and using for a utensil. For the kids meals you could do individual small tackle boxes, apple bushel baskets, a pail and shovel each filled with the corresponding meal. If you make individual boxes or bags for your guests you will want to assemble everything at home and pack it in your guests' box or bag. You can be as creative as you want. The idea is to get out there and explore your area while taking advantage of bringing along some terrific foods.

I am a firm believer that everyone eat the same meal, however, on picnics it is sometimes nice to have an adult meal and a kids meal. This allows you to have a romantic or exotic picnic and make the kids feel special at the same time. We would split the duty and one would make an adult meal and one would make a kid's meal. Each basket in the book has an idea for an adult meal and a kid's meal for four people, along with drinks and appetizers.

Packing for the Picnic

It is easiest to keep your picnic stuff all together in the garage or closet so that it is always ready at a moments notice.

Four items are necessary for the picnic:

- *Bag/basket with the supplies: Watch for these things to go on sale or get some from the party supply store to keep the picnic fun! Always keep plenty of supplies in your bag-you never know when your next picnic might be!*
- *Water cooler: Fill your water cooler with pop cans, bags of drinks, or bottles of beer (clean them first), add ice and water and its ready! Bring extra gallons of water to refill the cooler as needed. Don't forget the plastic cups.*
- *Soft-sided cooler bag for food: Invest in a soft side cooler bag to keep food cool. Buy some freezer packs to toss in along the sides of the bag or collect freezer bags from flower deliveries and if you have had children from the baby bag.*
- *Picnic Basket: A great picnic basket brings the fun and excitement into preparing and having a picnic. There are so many elegant, colorful, and fun baskets out there to choose from, your imagination is the limit.*

Cold Items

The how to of packing a cooler or picnic basket for cold items is to pack all of your cooled items in sealable bags or lidded plastic tubs. Line bottom of your cooler/basket with a tea towel, add your items and then another tea towel add a few sealable bags of ice, water filled frozen 2 liter pop bottles, or frozen juice boxes on top of everything (cold air sinks) and put the top on. You can drink the water from the 2 liter bottles as it melts. This should keep your items cool until ready to eat.

Hot Items

On the flip side for hot items pack all of your warmed items in sealable bags, lidded plastic tubs, or foil. Line the bottom of your cooler/basket with a tea towel, layer some oven heated bricks wrapped in foil, another tea towel on top and then your items and top the cooler (warm air rises). Start with items already the correct temperature and they should stay warm/cool until you are ready to eat!!

Locations for your Picnic

There are plenty of places out there to have your picnic-think outside the box. A picnic does not have to take weeks to plan; a spur of the moment picnic is as fun.

- *Look at all of your state and city parks. Even camping sites will have picnic tables and hiking trails and plenty of room to spread out.*
- *Checkout your local colleges and university's, some have duck ponds, so take a loaf of bread and feed the ducks while you are there.*
- *Do a search on Google for parks and gardens.*
- *Do not forget your GPS has a "Park/Garden" button.*

- After the kids finish their sport, have a picnic at that location.
- There are usually places to spread out a blanket after you have picked your fruit-and how fun to sit and eat your fruit you just picked.
- A lunch visit to dad at the office.
- A trip to the pool.
- A city or county fair or festival.
- On a rainy day your living room is a fun spot for a picnic. A checkered table cloth on the floor and you are ready.

Always be on the lookout for a good picnic location! Remember to always pack a blanket and some chairs just in case the ground is wet.

Stocking your picnic basket

Here is a quick checklist of items to always keep in your picnic pantry:
- Boxes of different size resalable bags
- Sealable plastic containers of various sizes
- Paper plates
- Plastic utensils
- Trash Bags
- Kitchen knife
- Kitchen towels
- Paper towels
- Picnic tablecloth
- Bottle/wine opener
- Salt/pepper
- Sugar/Coffee cream
- Plastic cups
- Plastic wine glasses
- Thermos
- Foil wrapped bricks (for weighing down in grilling and for heating)
- Foil
- Wet Wipes

Fill snack bag size zip locks for the road. This will also buy you a little more time once you get to the site. You can have one of the older kids assemble the bags. Just set out the number of bags (1 per child) and the ingredients to go in the bags. This is a good time to use paper bags and let the kids decorate their own bag with stickers. You can also, add a riddle to each bag for fun! If you have stamps, have one child stamp the first initial of each person attending the picnic and have an older child staple them to the bags you have selected.

- *Baby carrots and string cheese*
- *Mixed bag of cereal*
- *Almonds, chocolate chunks and dried cranberries*
- *Mini marshmallows and Cheerios*
- *Pretzels and M&M's*
- *Gummi's*
- *Dried fruit-figs, apricots, golden raisins, cranberries*
- *Beef Jerky/use the meatier "chunk" version for little mouths*
- *Honey and Peanut butter squares*
- *Yogurt covered raisins*
- *Pear slices with thin slices of ham wrapped around*
- *Ham wrapped cheese*
- *Quesadillas*
- *Hard boiled eggs*
- *Frozen portable yogurt*

For the ride home, Vicky and I usually gave them salsa and chips. Tear or cut the top half of plastic cups off, so little fingers can get down in there with a chip! Pour salsa into the cup and give each of them some chips and a cup of salsa-they do not want to share after playing all day. Feel free to substitute any of your children's favorite snacks for this idea. The main idea is to get a little something in their bellies for the ride home

Tia Marissa Salsa

1 can diced tomatoes and green chilies, mild
4 oz tomato sauce
1/2 lime juiced
1 c cilantro
1 clove garlic or 1 teaspoon garlic powder

2 teaspoon cumin
1 Anaheim peppers roasted, 2 for spicy
Salt
1/4 c onion

Combine all ingredients in a blender and blend until smooth. Yield 3 cups salsa

Spring

-Just living is not enough," said the
butterfly, "One must have sunshine, freedom
and a little flower." ~Hans Christian Anderson

Farmers Market Basket

Appetizer: Feta Onion Dip
Baguette sandwich with fresh vegetables, basil and mozzarella
Sweet Mixed Berries
Drink: Melon Vodka and Sprite
Kids menu: Peter Rabbit and Farmer McGregor Giant carrots with the green still attached, lettuce wraps filled with cheese and meat, ranch dip, mixed berries, orange juice

Fresh from the Garden Basket

Appetizer: Cherry Tomatoes stuffed with Basil and Salami
Grilled Asparagus wrapped with Black Forest Ham
Strawberries filled with chocolate chunks
Drink: Peach Bellini
Kids Menu: More Sprinkles Please! Kebobs with meat, cheese, and fruit, Ice cream cone cupcakes with white fluffy icing and sprinkles, mixed fruit juice

Georgian Basket

Appetizer: Goat and artichoke Dip
Sweet and Salty Fried Chicken
Oma's Potato Salad
Angle food Cake with blueberries and cream
Drink: Wheat Beer
Kids Menu: Hawaiian Delight Platter, Pineapple boats filled with fruit, meat and cheese skewers, angle food cake with pineapple cream cheese icing and pineapple juice.

The Fiesta Basket

Appetizer: Salsa and Chips
Cilantro Cream Fajita Wraps
Fresh Corn Salsa
Gammo Lisa's Pan de Polvo
Drink: Margarita
Kids Menu: Soft shell taco platter, sweet and spicy brownies and fizzy apple juice

Greek Flavors Basket

Appetizer: Almond Stuffed Dates
Lamb "fingers" with Mint Chimichurri sauce
Golden raisin couscous
Drink: Prickly Pear Vodka cosmos
Kids Menu: Huff and Puff Ham and Cheese Puffs, Strawberry/Raspberry Puffs, Watermelon slush

Feta Onion Dip

1 8oz block of cream cheese
4 oz of feta cheese, crumbled
4 sun dried tomatoes packed in oil, chopped
2 tablespoons cilantro, chopped
2 tablespoons red onion, chopped
2 tablespoons basil, chopped
Sliced radishes for dipping

Soften the cream cheese on the counter for 15 minutes. In a bowl use a fork and mash the crumbled feta into the cream cheese. You may have to add a splash of cream to soften the mixture. Stir in the chopped sun dried tomatoes. Scoop mixture into a bowl and top with chopped cilantro, red onion and basil. Serve with slices of radishes at room temperature.

To transport: Scoop dip into a Ziploc and then at the site spread your dip onto a paper plate and top with the cilantro, onion and basil. Place the radishes around the edge of the paper plate.

Baguette Sandwich
Sliced cherry tomatoes
Sliced radishes
Whole basil leaves
Sliced fresh mozzarella cheese
8 brown paper bags

Slice all of the baguettes open and spread each piece with some of the soft cheese of your choice. In each baguette place, 1 red leaf lettuce, slices of cherry tomatoes, slices of radishes, slices of mozzarella and top with whole basil leaves.

Wrap each sandwich in a brown paper bag and tie with a string. For a special effect put each persons name on a tag and attach to the string.

Sweet Mixed Berries

2 container of fresh strawberries, sliced
2container of blueberries
2 containers of raspberries
1/4 cup of sugar (or less depending on berry sweetness)
Chopped mint (or pineapple sage, if you can find it)
Toothpicks or small wooden forks for eating berries
4 small plastic cups

Tip: Bring a bowl of freshly whipped cream to pass around to dip berries!

Mix all of the berries in a bowl with the sugar and mint or the pineapple sage. Let set for 20 minutes to get the juices flowing.
To transport, pour all berries into a lidded plastic container and put in your cooler bag.
At the picnic, give each person a bag wrapped sandwich and a cup of berries with a toothpick for eating.

Melon Vodka Drink

4 oz Melon flavored vodka
16 oz sprite, cold
Melon slices

Mix the vodka and sprite in a glass add the melon slices and serve.

4 Giant Carrots with the greens still attached
4 bendable pieces of lettuce
4 pieces of ham
4 pieces of cheese
4 baggies potato chips
Ranch Dressing
Mixed berries

Wash and dry each lettuce leaf.   On top of the lettuce, place one piece of ham and one piece of cheese. Roll up lettuce roll and secure with a toothpick or fun skewer.

Serve on a paper plate with carrot, lettuce roll, a baggie of chips and ranch dressing to use for the dip and a cup of mixed berries.

Grilled Asparagus wrapped with Black Forest Ham

24 stalks of asparagus (4 per person)
12 pieces of black forest or Ardennes ham
Olive oil
Salt/Pepper

Preheat grill. Roll the stalks of asparagus in olive oil and salt and pepper.
Best way to do this is on a cookie sheet. Place asparagus on grill and grill
about 10-20 depending on the heat of the grill. Make sure the stalks are still
firm. Place 2 pieces of ham on a plate and top with 4 stalks of asparagus
and roll ham around stalks. Place seal side down on plate you intend to
transport to the picnic. Continue until all bundles are completed.

Cherry Tomatoes stuffed with Basil
24 cherry tomatoes
24 Basil leaves
24 pieces of feta cheese

Cut off the top and scoop out the centers of the cherry tomatoes. Fill each
tomato with a piece of feta cheese and put a basil leaf in each tomato.

Strawberries filled with chocolate chunks- 3 Strawberries per person
12 Strawberries, large ones
12 pieces of good quality chocolate chunks

Wash strawberries, thoroughly. Cut the green stem out of the strawberries
to create a small hole in the strawberry. Put 1 piece of chocolate chunk in
the middle of each berry. Prepare berries before leaving the house and put
in lidded plastic container.

Peach Bellini

5 oz champagne
1 oz peach nectar

This makes 1 serving so adjust according to your group size.
Pour the nectar into a champagne flute and then add the champagne, gently
stir. If you cannot find the peach nectar, try blending some frozen peach
slices in the blender.

Meat and Cheese Skewers
Meat cubes
Cheese cubes
Tomatoes
Strawberries
Skewer

Use 1 skewer and thread the meat, cheese, tomatoes, and strawberries on the skewer in an alternating fashion. If the skewer is too long, break it in half and use 2 skewers. Be sure to leave space at the bottom for little hands to hold onto the skewer.

Ice Cream Cone Cupcakes
1 box of cake mix (18.25 oz)
1 box 12 Jumbo Ice cream cone cups (with the flat bottom)
1 container of white icing
Sprinkles

Prepare cake mix according to package directions. Place the 12 cones in a cupcake pan. Pour the batter into each cone until about 2/3 full. The batter will rise and you do not want too many overflowing.   Place filled cones in the cupcake pan in the oven. Bake at 350-degree oven for about 15-20 minutes. Place on counter to cool. Once cooled ice with icing and decorate with sprinkles. To transport to the picnic site place cones in a box. If the box is too big, place cones towards the center of the box and wrap a sheet of wax paper around the outside of the cones (between the cones and the box) to keep in place during the travel period.

Goat Cheese and Artichoke Dip

4 ounces Goat cheese

1 cup canned Artichokes

1 teaspoon lime zest

1 juiced lime

salt and pepper to taste

Baby carrots, grape tomatoes, broccoli, blanched asparagus

In a food processor blend all ingredients until smooth and add salt and pepper to taste. The dip can be made the day ahead. Keep cool until picnic. Pack dip in a sealable container and vegetables in a zip bag.

Oma's Potato Salad

2 pounds new potato

1 cup pickles -- chopped

1/2 cup mayonnaise

2 teaspoons Dijon mustard -- good quality such as Grey Poupon

 2 tablespoons dill -- chopped

2 tablespoons pickle juice

2 teaspoons salt

1 teaspoon pepper

2 eggs -- boiled, optional

In a bowl mix pickles, mayonnaise, Dijon mustard, dill, pickle juice, salt and pepper and set aside. Add potatoes in a pot of cold water and bring to a boil until a knife inserted in the middle of one potato comes out clean. While the potatoes are cooking drop in the two eggs and cook for 10 minutes. Remove the eggs and run under cold water until cooled.   Drain the potatoes and add to the dressing.   You want to add the potatoes when they are hot, as they cool they will absorb the flavor of the dressing. Chop the eggs and add to the salad. Once the salad has cooled refrigerate until ready to pack. The potato salad can be made a day ahead, serve at room temperature.

Sweet and Salty Fried Chicken

8 pieces chicken -- Use your favorite
1 cup flour
2 eggs

1 cup buttermilk

oil
salt and pepper
honey

Bring chicken to room temperature. In one dish mix the flour with 2 teaspoon salt and 1 teaspoon pepper. In another dish whisk together the eggs and buttermilk. In a flat bottomed pan (preferably cast iron) heat in enough oil to reach the middle of the pan on med high until the oil reaches a temperature of 350. Dredge the chicken pieces in the flour, then egg mix, then flour again and into the oil. Repeat until pan is full (do not over crowd). Cook the chicken for 10 minutes on one side, flip and cook another 10 minutes on the other side.   Take the chicken out and drain on a paper towel. Season with salt immediately. Transport chicken in a paper bag as this will keep the chicken crisper longer. Keep chicken warm until picnic. At the picnic site drizzle chicken with honey.

Tip: If you put the chicken pieces in slowly it will allow the oil to come up to temperature as you add the next piece. You want to maintain an oil temperature of 350.

Angel Food Cake

1 1/2 cups egg whites (from about 12 large eggs)
1 cup granulated sugar
1 Pinch salt
1 teaspoon cream of tartar

1 1/2 teaspoons vanilla extract

3/4 cup flour
1/2 pint blueberries
1 cup whipped cream

Preheat oven to 350. In a mixer with a wire whisk attachment whisk egg whites and cream of tartar until soft peaks form. Add salt and vanilla and whisk until stiff peaks form. Do not over mix as the whites will become dry. Add sugar slowly and whisk until mixture is glossy and stiff. Fold in flour and pour into an un-greased angel food cake pan and bake for 30-35 minutes until top is golden brown and springs back to the touch. To keep the cake from deflating turn the cake still in the pan upside down on the neck of a wine bottle to cool. Run a knife around cake and un-mold. Up to this point can be done the day ahead. Serve with whipped cream and blueberries. Keep whipped cream cool until picnic.

1 pineapple
4 oz each cubed ham and your favorite cheese
1 loaf Hawaiian bread, found in deli section of your grocer
4 slices Angle food Cake
1/2 can cream cheese frosting
1 can crushed pineapple, drained
4 cans pineapple juice

Cut pineapple in quarters vertically (do not cut off leafy top). Cut out pineapple saving the top and skin to make a boat. Core pineapple fruit and cut into chunks. Pack boats and chunks in sealable bags. Skewer ham and cheese on small skewers. Pack in bags. Mix drained crushed pineapple and cream cheese frosting. Pack in a plastic container. Fill one quarter of the scooped out pineapple with the chunks of pineapple, stick skewered meat and cheese around the boat and a piece of bread on the side. Serve with 1 slice of angle food cake topped with pineapple frosting and pineapple juice.

Cilantro Cream Fajita Wraps

2 pounds flank steak
2 cups heavy cream
1 1/2 bunches cilantro
1 clove garlic
1 jalapeno

2 teaspoons salt
1 teaspoon pepper
2 cups Monterey jack cheese
8 flour tortilla

In a saucepan combine cream with garlic clove and bring to a simmer. Cook until cream is reduced by half, about 10-15 minutes. In the last 1 minute add the cilantro to blanch. In a blender combine hot cream, cilantro, jalapeno, salt and pepper and blend until smooth. Meanwhile, bring meat to room temperature and preheat grill on high. Season both sides of meat with salt and pepper and grill for 3-4 minutes per side. This will give you a medium rare center. Let meat rest for 10 minutes. At this point you can pack up the meat in tin foil and then in a sealable bag.

Tip: Save time by using an immersion blender to blend cream.

Pack cilantro cream, tortillas, and cheese into separate containers. Keep meat and cream warm. At your picnic site cut the meat against the grain. Lay out one tortilla and spread a few tablespoons of the cream down the center, place 3-4 strips of meat and about 1/4 cup of cheese and wrap. Repeat until you have made all 8.

Fresh Corn Salsa

2 ears fresh corn   1 small red onion
2 medium tomato's   2 limes -- juiced
1 pablano pepper   1 teaspoon honey
1/2 bunch cilantro   salt and pepper

Roast the corn and pablano pepper on the grill over high heat until browned
or in the oven under the broiler. Place the pepper in a plastic bag to steam.
When the corn is cool enough to handle cut the kernels off the cob. Seed
and de-vein the pepper and chop. Chop the tomato, cilantro and red onion.
Combine chopped ingredients into a bowl and stir in lime juice and honey.
Salt and pepper to taste. You can make this the day ahead.

Margarita

1 cup tequila
1 cup ginger ale or sprite
1 small limeade, frozen concentrate
1/4 cup Triple Sec liqueur
Ice
Mix tequila, limeade, triple sec. Pack in a leak proof container.
At picnic site in a pitcher mix tequila mix with ginger ale and
ice. Stir to combine and serve in fun plastic glasses.

Gammo Lisa's Pan de Polvo

4 cups flour
1 cup sugar + 1 cup sugar
2 cups shortening
2 teaspoons baking powder
2 egg whites
2 teaspoons cinnamon

Blend 1 cup sugar and eggs to until foaming. Mix flour, shortening
and baking powder in a separate bowl. Combine egg/sugar mixture to flour.
Knead about 10 minutes. Roll and cut into little bite size cookies. Bake 7-8
minutes at 350. In a small bowl mix 1 cup sugar and cinnamon. Once baked
gently roll cookies in cinnamon/sugar mix.

4 Tortillas
1/2 pound ground beef
1 packet taco seasoning
1 cup cheddar cheese
1/2 cup cherry tomatoes
1/4 cup cilantro
Sliced peppers, yellow, green, red
1 lime, quartered

In a skillet cook ground beef through. Add taco seasoning according to package directions.
Serve with assorted toppings. To transport to the picnic site: Place all tortillas in a piece of foil and place on a warm foil wrapped brick. Place each of the toppings in a separate zip lock.
At the picnic site place assorted toppings on platter and let each child pick what toppings they would like and place them on top of the tortilla.

Sweet and Spicy Brownies

1 package of brownie mix
1 container of chocolate icing
2 teaspoons Mrs. Dash Southwest Chipotle Seasoning

Make and bake brownies according to package directions. When brownies are cool, ice with you favorite icing. Sprinkle the seasoning on the iced brownies and serve.

To pack brownies, slice into squares or triangles and place in a plastic sealable container. Layer the brownies in the container by putting wax paper between the layers. Place brownies in container in the fridge to keep cold before the trip.

Fizzy Apple Juice

Cold Apple juice
Cold Sparkling water

In a small glass, pour half a glass of apple juice and top off with sparkling water to fill the cup ¾ full. Gently stir and enjoy. If time permits, make some frozen apple juice cubes in the freezer, dump them into a zip lock and transport in the cooler to the picnic site.

Almond Stuffed Dates with Cheese
16 Medjoul Dates
16 whole almonds
 8 oz Vermont aged cheddar or good quality parmesan cheese

Remove pits in dates by making a slit in one side and removing pit. Add almond where pit was.   Up to this point can be made the day ahead. Serve with slices of good Vermont aged cheddar or parmesan cheese.

Lamb "fingers" with Mint Chimichurri sauce

1 bunch mint	3/4 cup olive oil
2 cloves garlic	2 racks lamb—frenched and cut into chops
3 tablespoons red wine vinegar	salt and pepper
1 lemon juiced	

In a blender combine mint, garlic, red wine vinegar, and lemon juice, pulse to combine. While blender is running slowly add oil to emulsify. Pack in a plastic container. The sauce can be made a day ahead. Preheat grill on high heat. Brush lamb chops with olive oil and season with salt and pepper. Grill 2 minutes per side for medium rare. Serve with the mint chimichurri sauce. If you grill at home wrap the lamb chops in foil and then in a resalable plastic bag. Keep lamb warm until picnic. If you grill at your picnic site place chops in a plastic bag and add 3 tablespoons of oil and salt and pepper then grill at site.

Tip: A Frenched rack of lamb is where the meat and fat is cut away from the bone. Cutting into chops is cutting vertically between the bones.

Shortcut: Substitute good quality dressing for chimichurri such as Kens Caesar Salad Dressing

Golden Raisin Couscous

1 cup uncooked couscous	1/2 teaspoon salt -- omit if using chicken stock
	1 cup golden raisins
1 cup water or chicken stock	
1/4 cup butter	1/4 teaspoon cinnamon

In a sauce pan bring water or chicken stock to a boil and add salt. Mix in couscous and remove from heat and cover. Let stand until all the liquid has been absorbed. Fluff with a fork and add butter, raisins and cinnamon. Pack in a plastic container. Tip: The couscous needs to be made the day of the picnic, but can remain at room temperature until ready to serve.

Prickly Pear Vodka Cosmopolitan

1/2 cup Prickly pear vodka
1/4 cup Triple Sec liqueur
1/4 cup lime juice
1/4 cup cranberry juice
Ice
Sugar for rimming

Mix all ingredients into a sealable container and pack. At picnic site wet the edge of 4 fun glasses with lime juice and dip in sugar. Add ice and pour mix over ice. Serve.

Tip: substitute your favorite vodka for the prickly pear vodka, but if you can find the prickly pear vodka it is worth it!!

Puff the Magic Treats

2 sheets puff pastry -- Frozen section of grocery
4 slices ham
4 slices cheese
4 tablespoons raspberry or strawberry preserves

Preheat oven to 350. Lay out puff pastry and cut each sheet into 4 equal squares. On 4 squares lay out the ham and then top with the cheese. Wet 2 corners of each square; fold over to make a triangle and seal. On the other 4 spread one tablespoon of your child's favorite preserves. Wet 2 corners of each square; fold over to make a triangle and seal. Brush the top with a little melted butter or olive oil and bake for 15 minutes until puffed and golden brown. Pack in a plastic container.

Watermelon slush

8 cups watermelon -- seeded
1/4 cup powdered sugar
6 ounces lemonade, frozen concentrate

Chop 1/2 watermelon and place in a large bowl; cover and freeze. Reserve the rest for another use. Place half of frozen watermelon, powdered sugar, and concentrate in a blender and process until smooth. Transport to picnic spot in a plastic container in your soft sided cooler bag surrounded by ice packs or frozen gel packs. Serve to kids in fun plastic cup with a straw and spoon.

Summer

-Summer is not summer,
Unless there is ice cream
~Denise McMurry

Seafood Delight Basket

Appetizer: Tuna pea salad in roma tomatoes with a dollop of wasabi mayo
Smoked salmon on a baguette with cream cheese and dill
Skewered Grilled Shrimp and mango
Drink: Radler Beer
Kids Menu: Going Fishing, fish sticks on baguette, seashells pasta with seaweed, worms in dirt, pond water

A Basket from the Carolina's

Appetizer: Apple slices with mixed hard cheeses
Vinegar Pulled Chicken Sandwiches with pickled Jalapeño and Creamy Cole slaw
Homemade Potato chips
Strawberries with reduced balsamic sauce
Drink: New Belgium Abby
Kids Menu: Chicken on a Stick, Parmesan chicken popsicles, crazy ranch with favorite veggies, peanut butter chocolate balls. Flavored water-carbonated water with lemon, lime and orange slices

The Pacific Basket

Appetizer: Roasted Eggplant
Swordfish sandwiches with wasabi mayo
Ceviche on Cucumber
Peanut butter Chocolate Chunk Cookies
Drink: Sangria
Kids Menu: Brown Bears Cut out Bear sandwiches, peanut butter and chocolate chunk cookies, yahoo chocolate

Truly Louisiana Basket

Appetizer: Goat Cheese and Dill Topped Tomatoes
Oyster Po Boys with Louisiana Mayo
Spicy Cole Slaw
Peach Cobbler
Drink: Hard Lemonade
Kids Menu: Baked Potato Bar, Carmel Topped apples and apple cider

A Baja Basket

Appetizer: Guacamole with Corn Chips
Talipa Fish Taco's with Chipotle Sauce
Fruit skewers with whole milk yogurt, lime, chili dip
Drink: Mexican Beer
Kids Menu: Say CHEEEEEEEESE Basket, Ham Quesadillas, Broccoli with Cheese Dip and apple and cheddar skewers, orange drink

Tuna Pea Salad in Roma Tomatoes

1 can tuna fish, drained
1/4 cup peas, fresh, frozen or canned
3/4 cup mayonnaise
1/2 cup pickles, chopped
1/4 teaspoon pepper
1 1/2 teaspoon wasabi, less for less heat
4 Roma tomatoes, seeded

In a bowl combine tuna, peas, ½ cup mayonnaise, pickles, and pepper. Set aside. In another small bowl combine ¼ cup mayonnaise and wasabi. Stir to combine. Slice tomatoes in half and remove seeds and center pulp. Pack tuna salad in a sealable container, wasabi mayonnaise in a separate container and tomatoes in a zip bag. At picnic site fill each half with tuna salad and top with a dollop of wasabi mayonnaise.

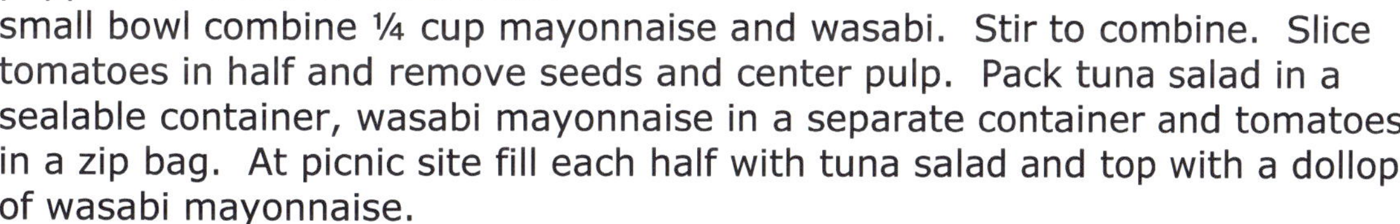

Smoked Salmon on a Baguette with Cream Cheese and Dill

1 baguette, cut into 4 pieces
8 oz smoked salmon
4 oz cream cheese
1 small bunch dill
1 small bunch chives
Romaine lettuce

Slice baguette pieces horizontally and spread each bottom piece with cream cheese, top with 2 oz smoked salmon, a few sprigs of dill and chives and lettuce. Wrap each sandwich in parchment or brown paper and tie with a ribbon or jute.

Skewered Grilled Shrimp and Mango

4 long skewers
1 mango, seeded and chopped into cubes
1/2 pound cooked large shrimp

Skewer shrimp and mango by placing each cube of mango inside the crook of each shrimp. Repeat until the skewer is full. Grill over high heat just until warm and grill marks are achieved. Sprinkle with pepper.

Radler Beer
2 wheat beers
4 cups orange soda

In a tall glass mix 1/2 of a beer and 1 cup of soda. Serve

Fish Sticks on Baguette

1/2 cup mayonnaise
1/4 cup pickles
2 teaspoons dill
1/2 lemon, juiced

8 fish sticks
4 small baguettes

In a small bowl combine mayonnaise, pickles, dill, and lemon juice. Cook fish sticks. On each baguette place a few teaspoons tartar sauce and 2 fish sticks. Wrap in fun paper or parchment and tie with jute. Keep sandwiches cool until ready to eat. For fun attach a plastic hook or bobber with a name tag to each sandwich.

Seashell Pasta with Seaweed

1/2 box seashell pasta
1/4 cup butter
1/2 cup parmesan cheese
3 tablespoons chopped basil
In a pot of salted boiling water cook pasta until al dente. Drain water and mix in butter, parmesan cheese, and basil. Pack into a sealable plastic container until ready to serve. The basil will darken from the heat of the pasta, making it look more like seaweed.

Worms in Dirt

4 individual cups of chocolate pudding
12 gummy worms
8 chocolate cookies
4 baggies

In each baggie crush 2 cookies and add 3 gummy worms. Pack baggies and pudding cups. At picnic site give each child one baggie and one cup of pudding to decorate their worms and dirt.

Pond Water
Any blue juice

Apple Slices with Mixed Hard Cheeses

2 apples, cored and sliced
Mixed sliced cheese, i.e. aged cheddar, white cheddar, parmesan, smoked Gouda

Vinegar Pulled Chicken Sandwiches with pickled Jalapeño and Creamy Cole slaw

For the roasted chicken:
1 whole chicken
1/2 cup butter, softened
3 tablespoons mixed fresh herbs
salt and pepper

For the Cole Slaw
1 cup mayonnaise
3 tablespoons apple cider vinegar
1 teaspoon sugar
1/2 teaspoon salt
1/4 teaspoon pepper

2 cups green cabbage, chopped
2 cups red cabbage, chopped
1 cup carrot, grated
1/2 cup scallion, chopped,

For the chicken dressing:
1 tablespoon course black pepper
1 tablespoon salt
1 teaspoon sugar
1 cup apple cider vinegar
1 jar pickled jalapeno peppers
4 whole wheat bread buns

Shortcut: Substitute one store bought rotisserie chicken for the chicken and 1 bag precut cabbage for the 4 cups cabbage

Preheat oven to 350. In a bowl combine butter and herbs and mix. Rinse chicken under cold water and pat dry. Run your finger under the skin to separate the skin from the meat. Push the butter mixture under the skin so that the meat is evenly coated on the breast and legs. Season the outside of the chicken with salt and pepper and roast for 1-1 1/2 hours until a meat falls easily from bone. Meanwhile for the cole slaw in a bowl whisk mayonnaise, 3 tablespoon apple cider vinegar, sugar, 1/2 teaspoon salt and 1/4 teaspoon pepper. Add the green and red cabbage, carrot and scallion to the bowl and toss to coat. Pack Cole slaw in plastic container and refrigerate until ready to pack.   Once the chicken has cooled remove skin and discard. Pull meat from the bone and shred into a large bowl. In a small bowl whisk the remaining 1 cup apple cider vinegar, pepper, salt and sugar and pour over the chicken and toss to coat. Pack chicken in a plastic container and refrigerate until ready to pack.   This can be done the night before. At your picnic site spoon chicken and coleslaw onto the wheat bun and top with pickled jalapeno peppers, serve.

Potato chips

2 baking potato
Oil
Salt

In a deep sauce pan add enough oil to go 1/2 the way up the side. Preheat oil to 350. Slice potato thin. When oil has reached 350 degrees fry potatoes in small batches until golden brown and crispy. Remove to a paper towel and salt immediately. Pack the chips in a brown paper school lunch bag or a brown paper grocery bag.

Shortcut: Substitute good quality store bought potato chips

Strawberries with Reduced Balsamic Sauce

2 pints strawberries
2 cups balsamic vinegar
1 teaspoon sugar

In a small saucepan combine the sugar and balsamic vinegar. Bring to a boil and cook until the liquid has reduced by 2/3. This can be done the day ahead. Once it is cool it should be thick. Just before you leave for the picnic hull the strawberries and pack them. At the picnic site add strawberries to a bowl and drizzle balsamic syrup over the top and serve.

Parmesan Chicken Popsicles

2 boneless skinless chicken breasts cut into strips
1 cup bread crumbs
1/2 cup parmesan cheese
1 cup milk
1 egg
3 tablespoons butter
3 tablespoons olive oil
6 popsicle sticks or fun skewers

In a small bowl combine bread crumbs and cheese. In another small bowl whisk the milk and eggs. Dredge chicken in milk mixture and then in bread crumbs making sure the bread crumbs cover all. Heat oil and butter in a skillet and cook chicken until golden brown on both sides about 4 minutes per side. Insert Popsicle sticks in each chicken piece. Pack chicken in a plastic container.

Crazy Ranch with favorite veggies

1/2 cup ranch
3-4 drops of your favorite food coloring
Carrots, tomatoes, sugar snap peas, broccoli

Mix ranch and food coloring. Pack into a plastic container. Pack veggies in a separate bag. At picnic site give each child a few veggies and 2-3 tablespoons of ranch.

Peanut Butter Chocolate Balls
1 cup peanut butter
1/4 cup powdered milk
1/4 cup powdered sugar
2 tablespoons honey
4 oz milk chocolate

Mix peanut butter, powdered milk, powdered sugar and honey. If it is to
sticky add more milk. Form into balls.   Melt the chocolate in the microwave
being careful not to over heat. (See Chocolate Dipped Strawberries for
tempering).   Roll peanut butter balls in melted chocolate and place in
refrigerator to cool and harden. Pack in a lidded plastic container.

Roasted Eggplant Dip

2 eggplant
1 clove garlic
1 lemon, juiced
4 pita pockets
1/4 cup olive oil

Preheat grill on medium.   Grill eggplant until soft, 20-30 minutes.   Or preheat oven 375. Place eggplant on cookie sheet and roast in oven until soft, about 30-40 minutes. When cool enough to handle slice eggplant in half and scrape out fruit leaving skin behind. Discard skin. Process fruit with lemon juice, olive oil, garlic clove and salt and pepper to taste. Cut pita into wedges (about 12 per pita). Pack this into a plastic container and serve with pita wedges or crackers of your choice. The dip can be made ahead and refrigerated, but serve at room temperature.

Swordfish Sandwiches with Wasabi Mayo

2 8oz Swordfish steaks
1/2 teaspoon chili powder
1/2 teaspoon garlic powder
1/2 teaspoon salt

1 cup mayonnaise
3 tablespoon wasabi
1 cup fresh spinach chopped
2 tomatoes sliced

1/2 teaspoon pepper

Sliced red onion
4 cibiatta bread

Preheat grill on high. Mix chili powder, garlic powder, salt, and pepper and sprinkle over steaks. Grill on med high heat for 3-4 minutes per side. In a small bowl mix the mayonnaise and wasabi.
Either before you leave or at picnic site layer half a swordfish steak, spinach, onion and tomatoes on the bread. Spread wasabi mayonnaise on bun and top. Wrap in butcher paper or parchment paper. For a fun addition tie with jute or a colorful ribbon.

Ceviche on Cucumber

1 lb shrimp, raw, shelled, de-veined
2 lemons
3 limes
Salt and pepper

1 tomato chopped
2 green onions chopped
3 tablespoon cilantro chopped
2 avocado chopped
1 cucumber, sliced

Chop shrimp into bite sized pieces. In a plastic container combine the shrimp, juiced lemons and juiced limes. Let set for 30 minutes or until shrimp turn pink. Mix in tomato, green onions, cilantro, avocado and salt and pepper to taste. Pack in a plastic container. This can be done the day ahead. Serve 4-5 cucumber slices to a plate topped with ceviche.

Sangria

1 lime, sliced
1 lemon, sliced
1 orange, sliced
1 cup pineapple with juice, cubed
1 apple, cubed (optional)
1 cup dark rum
1 bottle dry red wine
1 cup orange juice

In a pitcher or thermos combine lime, lemon, orange, pineapple and pineapple juice, apple and rum. Let this steep until you are ready to pack for the picnic. Slightly mash the fruit, add the red wine and orange juice. At picnic site fill a glass with sangria and a colorful fun pick to eat the fruit.

Peanut Butter Chocolate Chunk Cookies

1 1/2 sticks butter -- softened	2 cups flour
1/2 cup smooth peanut butter	1 teaspoon baking soda
1 cup brown sugar	1/2 teaspoon baking powder
1/2 cup white sugar	1/2 teaspoon salt
2 egg	8 oz chocolate chunks
1 teaspoon vanilla	

Preheat oven to 350. Cream butter, brown sugar, white sugar and peanut butter in a mixing bowl fitted with a paddle attachment until fluffy, about 3 minutes. Add eggs and vanilla and cream until combined. Sift together dry ingredients and combine. Do not over mix, but only mix until the dry ingredients are combined. Add Chocolate chunks. Spoon out onto a cookie sheet and bake for 10-12 minutes until the outside is beginning to set and the center looks a little underdone.   This can be done the day ahead.

Beary Good Sandwiches

8 slices Bread
4 slices ham
4 Slices cheese -- your child's favorite
Small tomato
Mayonnaise
Raisins

Spread mayonnaise on bread and put in one slice of ham and cheese. Top with another slice of bread. Use a bear cookie cutter to cut out sandwiches. You can have the kids decorate raisins for the eyes and buttons and a small slice of tomato for the mouth.

Desert

Giant Peanut Butter Chocolate Chunk Cookies (see recipe above)

Drink

Chilled Yoo-hoo

Tip: Peanut butter and jelly for meat and decorate with chocolate pieces.

Dill Goat Cheese Tomatoes

2	large tomato	2 teaspoons olive oil
4	ounces goat cheese	salt and pepper
2	tablespoons dill, chopped	

Combine softened goat cheese and chopped dill. Add salt and pepper to taste. At picnic site slice tomatoes into thick slices. Spread goat cheese mix into top of tomato slice and garnish with a drizzle of olive oil and pepper. Alternatively you could heat these over a grill for 2 minutes to soften the cheese. Then top with pepper and olive oil.

Oyster Po Boys with Spicy Sauce

16 raw oysters

1/2 cup milk

1/2 cup cornmeal seasoned with salt and pepper

Oil

2 c sliced lettuce

2 tomatoes sliced

1 cup mayo

3 teaspoon Louisiana hot sauce

4 Hoagie rolls

In a flat bottomed pan pour enough oil to go ¼ of the way up your pan. Heat on medium high heat until oil reaches a temperature of 350. Meanwhile dredge oysters the in milk and then cornmeal and fry until golden brown on both sides. Cook oysters the day of the picnic. In a small bowl mix mayo and Louisiana hot sauce. At home or at picnic site spread spicy sauce liberally on rolls and top with 4 oysters, lettuce and tomato. Wrap in parchment paper and pack. For added fun and color tie with jute or colorful ribbon.

Peach Cobbler

1/2 cup butter
1 cup flour
1 cup white sugar
1 teaspoon baking powder
1/2 cup milk
1/2 cup sour cream
2 cups fresh peaches

Preheat oven to 350. Place butter in an 9x9
glass or ceramic baking dish. Place dish in
oven until butter is melted. In a medium
bowl, combine flour sugar and baking
powder. Mix well, and then stir in milk and
sour cream. Spoon mixture into baking
dish, on top of melted butter. Pour peaches
over flour mixture.
Bake in preheated oven for 50 to 60
minutes, until peaches are bubbly and crust
is lightly browned.

Homemade Hard Lemonade

4 cups lemonade
8 oz dark rum
1 lemon sliced

Mix lemonade and rum and pack in a thermos or sealable drink container. At
picnic site fill glass with ice and pour in lemonade. Garnish with lemon slices.

Baked Potato Bar

2 baking potatoes
Sour cream
Butter
Cheese
Chopped chives
Bacon Bits

Shortcut:
You can microwave potatoes wrapped in a tea towel until soft

Preheat oven to 350. Wrap potatoes in tin foil and bake in oven for 1 hour minutes or until a knife inserted in middle comes out easily. . Bring warm potatoes, sour cream, butter, cheese and chives to picnic site and set out on table for children to top potatoes as they wish. For added fun tie foil wrapped potatoes in ribbon or string with a name tag for each child.

Carmel Topped Apples

3 apples cored and sliced
1 container caramel apple dip
1/2 c mini chocolate morsels
3 tablespoon nuts (optional)

In a plastic container lay apples just overlapping. Heat dip in the microwave just until spoonable. Drizzle caramel over apples and top with chocolate chips and nuts. Serve

Drink

Apple Cider

Guacamole with Corn Chips

3 avocados, ripe	2 tablespoon lime juice
1 teaspoon chili powder, pref. Ancho	3 tablespoons cilantro chopped, optional
1 teaspoon salt	1 bag corn chips

In a plastic container coarsely mash avocado with chili powder and salt. Mix in lime juice. Adjust seasoning to taste. Serve with corn chips.

Tilapia Fish Taco's with Chipotle Sauce

4 tilapia filets or similar white fish	1 cup mayo
1 teaspoon chili powder, pref ancho	2 tablespoon chopped chipotle en adobe, on Spanish aisle in grocery
1 teaspoon salt	4 flour tortillas
2 cup shredded cabbage	

Preheat grill on high. Slice tilapia filets in half lengthwise, season with chili powder and salt. Grill on med high 3-4 minutes per side. At this point wrap in tin foil and pack. In a small plastic container mix mayo and chopped chipotle en adobe. Add more chipotle for hotter sauce and less for a milder. Pack fish, sauce, cabbage and tortillas keeping fish warm and chipotle mayo cold. At picnic site lay out one tortilla and top with 2-3 tablespoons of the chipotle sauce, 2 pieces of fish and a heap of cabbage. Wrap and serve.

Fruit Skewers with Yogurt Dip

1 pint strawberries	2 c whole milk yogurt
1 apple chopped into bite sized pieces	3 tablespoons lime juice
2 bananas, sliced	1/2 teaspoon lime zest

1 cup Grapes
2 mangos, cubed

1/4 cup sugar
1/2 teaspoon chili powder
8 4 inch skewers

In a sealable container mix yogurt, lime juice and zest, sugar, and chili powder. Keep yogurt cool. Skewer all the fruit. Pack in a lidded plastic container. At picnic site serve 2 skewers per guest and a little dipping sauce.

Ham Quesadillas

4 tortillas
6 slices ham
2 cups shredded cheese

Lay out 2 tortillas and top with ½ cup of cheese on each. Layer 3 slices of ham on each tortilla and top with remaining cheese. Top with remaining tortilla and grill in a skillet or on heated grill until cheese is melted. Cut into wedges. Pack these in foil and then in a plastic bag

Broccoli with Cheese Dip

8oz cubed Velveeta
1/2 cup mild salsa
1/4 cup chopped cilantro

Melt the cheese and salsa mixture in the microwave, stirring at 2 minute intervals until cheese is comppletly melted. Stir in chopped cilantro and pour into container to take to picnic site.

Apple and Cheddar Skewers

2 apples, cut into bite sized chunks
1 cup cheddar cheese, cut into bite sized chunks
1/2 lemon
8 small skewers

Skewer apples and cheese and pack into a lidded plastic container. Squeeze lemon juice over top to keep apples from turning brown.

Fall

Everyone must take time to sit and watch
the leaves turn.
~Elizabeth Lawrence

The Asian Basket

Appetizer: Spring Rolls
Chicken lettuce wraps
Asian Spiked fruit Kabobs
Drink: Red Lotus
Kids: The Panda Basket, Brown bread and white bread sandwiches made with chicken, grass and lettuce, bamboo sticks and bacon ranch, fruit kebabs, juice boxes

A Parisian Basket

Ham and Cheese Quiche
Roasted Mushroom, onion, and Goat Cheese Quiche
Basil, Pear Salad
Chocolate Dipped Strawberries
Drink: Pommeau
Kids Menu: The Eiffel Tower: Grilled ham and cheese sandwich, mini skewers of cherry tomatoes and strawberries, apple cider to drink

The Atlantic Basket

Appetizer: Herb bundles and dip
Chicken salad on peach half
Parmesan Cheese puffs
Sliced mangos, peaches and oranges in an orange shell
Drink: Mijoto,
Kids Menu: A Peach of a Meal Tortilla wraps, flavor you own chips, Peaches in yogurt, Peach Gummies

A Steakhouse Basket

Appetizer: Mozzarella Caprazi
Steak, Cole Slaw Wraps with White Bean Puree
Roasted Garlic Tomatoes
Coffee Brownies
Drink: New Belgium Spring Board
Kids Menu: Dinner in a Bag Chunks of steak and cherry tomatoes, brownie wrapped in parchment, Drink: lemonade juice bags

Beer and Brats Basket

Brats
Sauerkraut
Bacon Mustard Potato Salad
Apple Strudel
Drink: Weizen Beer
Kids Menu: Pigs in a Picnic Blanket Hot dogs rolled in crescent rolls with ketchup faces, Dirty cucumbers, Bug juice

Spring Rolls

1/2 pound small shrimp
1 package rice noodles
3 carrots
8 dried rice paper - available in most supermarkets in the Asian aisle

2 cups baby spinach
2 avocado
1 cucumber
1 bunch mint

1 bunch cilantro

Shortcut: substitute sashimi for rolls.

Cook shrimp in a pot of boiling salted water until they are pink. When cool peel and cut crosswise in half and set aside. Put rice noodles into a heat proof bowl and pour boiling water over them and let sit for 15 minutes or until soft. Cut carrots and cucumber into sticks 3 inches shorter than the rice paper. Slice the avocado. Pull the leaves from the mint and cilantro. You want to prepare your ingredients and place them in assembly line style. Once all the ingredients are prepared run one sheet of the rice paper at a time under warm water.   As they start to soften stack them. I work with 3-4 sheets at a time.   Pull one soft sheet from your stack and place about 1/8 cup of rice noodles down the center, as if making a taco, then on top of that place some shrimp in a row, then the carrot, cucumber, avocado, then a little mint and cilantro. Tuck in the ends and roll. The rice paper should stick to itself. When you are done stack them into a plastic tub and move to the next. Keep cool until picnic. Serve with the Ginger Lime dipping sauce and Hoi sin sauce.

Chicken Lettuce Wrap

For the sauce:
1 tablespoons mirin
1/4 cup soy sauce
2 tablespoons rice wine vinegar
1 tablespoon cornstarch

1 teaspoon fresh ginger, chopped
1 pound Chicken -- finely chopped
1 can water chestnuts, chopped
1 can bamboo shoots, chopped
1/4 cup carrots – shredded

1 tsp sesame oil

2 tsp oil, olive or any sauté oil
3 cloves garlic, chopped

8 Lettuce cups -- preferably butter lettuce but iceberg substitutes nicely

Ginger Lime Sauce -- recipe follows
Prepared Hoi Sin Sauce -- found in the Asian section of you grocery

In a small bowl combine soy sauce, mirin, rice wine vinegar, cornstarch and sesame oil and set aside. Heat wok or pan on high heat. Add oil until a little smoke comes off the oil and add the garlic and ginger. Sauté for 2 minutes until both become soft. Add chicken and cook until chicken is cooked through. Add water chestnuts, bamboo shoots, and carrot and sauté until all water is cooked off. To the pan add the combined sauce and sauté until the sauce thickens. It should only take 2-3 minutes. Pack the chicken into a sealable plastic tub. Separate the lettuce leaves from the head. You should end up with about 8 small cups about the size of your hand. Pack these in a sealable bag or plastic tub.   Keep chicken warm and lettuce cool until picnic.

For the Ginger Lime Sauce: Combine 1 teaspoon grated ginger, 1/2 teaspoon grated garlic (one small clove), 3 tablespoon fish sauce, 1/4 c lime juice, a pinch of pepper flakes. Also pack this a small sealable container.

Asian Spiked Fruit Kabobs

For the reduction
1 1/2 cups water
3/4 cup sugar
1 stalk lemon grass
1 teaspoon coriander seed -- slightly crushed
5 peppercorns

8 Skewers
1/2 pineapple
3 Asian pear (or bartlet)
1 pint strawberries
1 can lychee fruit (optional) found on the Asian Aisle
1/2 small bunch mint

Drain lychee fruit and reserve 1/2 of the liquid. For the reduction: in a small sauce pan combine ½ cup reserved lychee liquid, water, sugar, lemon grass, coriander seed and peppercorns and cook until reduced by half. Set aside to cool. The reduction can be done the day ahead. This should take about 15 minutes, just enough time to skewer your fruit. Cut pineapple and pear into chunks. If strawberries are large cut them in half. Skewer all of the fruit putting a mint leaf between each piece of fruit. Place skewered fruit into a plastic tub and pour cooled liquid over fruit. This can be done the night before.   Serving suggestion: Bring along the frond (or leafy top) half of your pineapple and push skewers into pineapple for serving. Serve left over sauce next to fruit.

Red Lotus Cocktail

1 cup Vodka
3/4 cup Lychee Juice (from canned lychee)
2 cup Cranberry Juice
4 Lychee fruit

In a sealable container mix Vodka, lychee juice and cranberry juice. At your picnic site fill 4 fun glasses with ice and pour in mix. Alternatly sugar the rims of 4 glasses with a little lime juice and shake the cocktail with ice and strain into glasses. Slide one lychee on each glass.Serve

For the sandwiches:

4 slices wheat bread

4 slices white bread

4 slices sliced chicken lunch meat

4 small pieces lettuce

1 small bunch chives

8 celery sticks, leaves attached

1 cup ranch

1 slice bacon, cooked crispy and cooled

Mixed cubed fruit

8 small skewers

On four pieces of bread layer; one slice chicken, one piece lettuce, a few chives and top with bread. Pack in sealable bags. Mix crispy bacon with ranch and pack. Skewer fruit on skewers and pack in a lidded plastic container. At picnic site each child gets one sandwich, 2 celery stalks, ¼ cup ranch and 2 skewers on their plate. Alternately you can pack individual Chinese take out containers or decorated paper bags for each picnicker.

Tip: The bacon can be cooked the day ahead.

Ham and Cheese Quiche

1 1/4 cup flour	4 eggs
1 teaspoon salt	1 pint 1/2 and 1/2
1 teaspoon sugar	1/4 lb ham or procuitto
6 tablespoon butter, cold	1 1/2 cups baby Swiss

Preheat oven to 350. For the crust: in a bowl mix flour, salt and sugar. Cut in cold butter until butter is broken into pea size balls. Bring dough together with 3-4 tablespoon ice water. Chill for 30 minutes. Roll out on a floured surface and fit into 9" pie shell. In another bowl whisk eggs and 1/2 and 1/2. In your pie shell layer the ham first and then cheese on top. Pour egg mixture over and bake for 45 minutes or until just set, but jiggles in the middle. Let cool. I have found the easiest way to transport 2 quiches is to put a plastic plate upside down on one quiche and place the other quiche on top of the plastic plate.   Place stack on top of a large tea towel and gather corners and tie with kitchen string. Keep quiche warm until ready to serve.

Shortcut: Make both crusts at once and mix both egg mixtures at the same time and divide between the two crusts

Roasted Mushroom, Onion and Goat Cheese Quiche

1 1/4 cup flour	4 eggs
1 teaspoon salt	1 pint 1/2 and 1/2
1 teaspoon sugar	1/2 lb mixed mushrooms, shitake, crimini, oyster, enokii, white, chopped
6 tablespoon butter, cold	1/2 sweet onion chopped
	3 tablespoon olive oil
	4 oz Goat Cheese

Preheat oven to 350. For the crust: in a bowl mix flour, salt and sugar. Cut in cold butter until butter is broken into pea size pieces. Bring dough

Shortcut: Substitute pre-made pie shells for the crust.

together with 3-4 tablespoon ice water. Chill for 30 minutes. Roll out on a floured surface and fit into 9" pie shell. On a cookie sheet mix the mushrooms and onions and drizzle with olive oil. Roast in oven for 20 minutes. In another bowl whisk eggs and 1/2 and 1/2. In your pie shell layer the mushrooms and onions, pour egg mixture over and crumble goat cheese on top. Bake for 45 minutes or until just set, but jiggles in the middle.

Basil Pear Salad
2 pears
1/4 cup basil, chopped
1/4 cup parmesan cheese, thinly sliced
4 cups baby spinach
1/4 cup balsamic vinegar
4 tablespoons olive oil
Salt and pepper

In a small leak proof container mix vinegar, oil, salt and pepper to taste. Pack basil, parmesan cheese and spinach separately. At picnic site core and slice pears. On the plate place 1 cup spinach and top with 4 slices of pear, and a few slices of parmesan cheese. Sprinkle basil over and top with balsamic vinaigrette.

Chocolate Dipped Strawberries

12 large strawberries
8 oz good quality dark chocolate

Wash strawberries and dry thoroughly. Heat chocolate in a double boiler or in microwave until almost all the chips have melted. At that point stir until the rest of the chips melt, this will give you chocolate that is tempered. Do not dip strawberries in the chocolate until the chocolate is body temperature to the

touch.   Dip strawberries in chocolate and place on a wax lined cookie sheet. When you have finished with all the strawberries place the cookie sheet in refrigerator to cool the chocolate. Pack in a lidded plastic container. Make sure to do this the day of the picnic. Keep strawberries cool.

Pommeau

6 oz Calvados (Apple Brandy)
2 c apple juice
2 c sprite or ginger ale

In a thermos mix calvados and apple juice. At picnic site fill a tumbler with ice, top with 1/2 cup apple juice mix and 1/2 cup sprite. Serve

Grilled ham and cheese sandwich

8 pieces white bread
4 pieces ham
8 pieces cheese
4 tablespoons butter

Butter each side of bread. With the butter side down layer cheese, ham, cheese on 4 slices. Top with the other 4 slices of bread butter side out. Heat sauté pan on med-high heat. Sauté sandwiches until golden brown and cheese is melted.

Skewers of cheery tomatoes and strawberries

1 pint cherry tomatoes
12 strawberries
4 long skewers
Make skewers by alternating tomatoes and strawberries.

Drink

Apple cider

Herb Bundles and Dipping Sauce

12 baby spinach leaves
12 large basil leaves
12 sprigs dill
12 sprigs mint
12 chives

Dipping Sauce
1/2 cup peanut butter
3 tablespoon soy sauce
1 teaspoon grated ginger
1/2 teaspoon grated garlic
1 teaspoon rice wine vinegar

In a small bowl whisk peanut butter, soy sauce, ginger, garlic, rice wine vinegar and 2 teaspoons water. Pack in a lidded plastic container. Lay out 1 spinach leaf and inside that place 1 basil leaf, 1 dill sprig, and 1 mint sprig. Roll up herbs and tie with one chive. To pack: wet a paper towel and ring out extra water roll all herb bundles in the damp paper towel and place in a zip bag. Keep refrigerated until you are ready to pack. Serve with dipping sauce.

Chicken Salad on a Peach

1 cup mayonnaise
1/4 cup honey Dijon mustard
2 teaspoon rosemary, chopped
1/2 teaspoon salt
1/2 teaspoon pepper

2 chicken breast sautéed and cubed
3 scallions chopped
1/2 cup celery, chopped
2 cups red grapes, sliced in half
1/2 cup sliced almonds
4 peaches, sliced and pitted

In a large bowl combine mayonnaise, Dijon mustard, rosemary and salt and pepper. To that toss chicken breasts, scallions, celery and grapes. Pack in a plastic container. This can be done the day ahead. Keep chicken salad cool until ready to serve. At the picnic site mix almonds into the chicken salad and serve mounded on peach halves.

Parmesan Cheese Puffs

2 sheets puff pastry

4 tablespoon butter
1/2 cup parmesan cheese

Preheat oven to 350. Layout
both puff pastry sheets and
brush with butter. Sprinkle
cheese over one sheet and
top with the other sheet
butter side down and press
together to seal. Cut into 12
strips and twist each strip and
place on a cookie sheet.
Bake for 15 minutes or until
golden brown.   Pack in a
lidded plastic container. At
the picnic site you can serve
these upright in a fun cup
decorated with ribbon or jute.

Fruit Cups

1 mango, pitted and chopped
1 peach chopped
4 oranges
2 tablespoon honey

Slice 1 inch off each orange. With a spoon carefully remove orange from shell
without damaging the shell. Chop two of the oranges and mix them with the
chopped mango and peach. In a small bowl squeeze the juice from the 2 remaining
oranges and whisk with honey. Pour over the mixed fruit and spoon back into
orange shells. Pack in a plastic container. The shells can be decorated with ribbon
or topped with a umbrella pick at the picnic site.

Mojito

1 cup rum
1/2 cup lime juice
1/2 cup simple syrup
2 cups carbonated water
2 teaspoon mint leaves

In a sealable container muddle (mash together) lime juice, simple
syrup, and mint leaves. Add rum. At picnic site fill glasses with ice
add 1/2 cup of mix and 1/2 cup of carbonated water, top with a lime.

Tip: Simple
syrup is a
mixture of
equal parts
water and
sugar
heated until
the sugar
dissolves
and then
cooled.

Tortilla Wraps

4 small tortillas
4 oz cream cheese
8 slices ham
4 large pickles, dried

Lay tortillas out and spread with cream cheese. Top with ham and pickles.
Roll tortillas and seal with a little cream cheese and place seam side down.
Cut into 1 inch wheels. Pack in a lidded plastic container and refrigerate until
you are ready to pack.

Flavor your own Chips

4 baggies plain potato chips
Assorted dried seasoning: dried Ranch, taco seasoning, dried bbq seasoning,
popcorn cheese

Give each child 1 bag of chips and allow them to pick the seasoning. About 1
teaspoon of the seasoning should season a sandwich bag full of chips.

Peaches in Yogurt

2 peaches, chopped
4 small containers yogurt

Mix yogurt and peaches and serve. This can be done at picnic site or before
you leave and then packed into a lidded plastic container.

Mozzarella Caprazi

2 balls fresh mozzarella
2 medium tomatoes
8-10 basil leaves
2 tablespoons balsamic vinegar
1 tablespoon olive oil
Salt and pepper

At picnic site on a plate slice mozzarella and tomatoes 1/8 inch thick. Fan on a platter by alternating mozzarella-tomato ect. Place basil leaves on every other stack. Drizzle with balsamic vinegar, olive oil and salt and pepper. Keep mozzarella cheese cool until ready to serve.

Steak and Cole Slaw Wraps with White Bean Puree

For the cole slaw:
2 cups shredded cabbage
1 pablano pepper chopped
1/2 red onion chopped
3 tablespoon olive oil
1/4 cup lime juice
2 tablespoon fish sauce, optional
1 teaspoon sugar
1 teaspoon salt
1 teaspoon pepper
2 teaspoon chipotle en adobe

For the white bean puree
2 cloves garlic, chopped
2 tablespoon olive oil
1 can navy beans, drained
1 teaspoon thyme
2 tablespoon lemon juice

1 8 oz rib eye or NY strip steak
4 burrito size tortillas

For the cole slaw: In a medium bowl whisk together olive oil, lime juice, fish sauce, sugar, salt, pepper, chipotle en adobe. Toss in cabbage, pepper and onion. Pack and refrigerate until ready to assemble. This can be done the day ahead.

For the white bean puree heat olive oil in a sauté pan, add garlic and sauté until soft, add beans, thyme and salt and pepper to taste. Mash bean while cooking until about half of the beans are mashed. Remove from heat and stir in lemon juice. Pack until ready to assemble. This can be done the day ahead. Heat grill on high heat. Salt and pepper both sides of steak and grill until medium rare or a thermometer reads 145 degrees. The steaks can be grilled at the picnic site or at home. If grilled at home wrap in tin foil and a sealable bag and keep warm until picnic.

At picnic site slice steak into thin slices across the grain. Lay out a tortilla and spread on the white bean puree, top with 3-4 slices of the steak and cole slaw. Wrap tortilla and serve.

Garlic and Herb Roasted Tomatoes

2 pint grape tomatoes
2 cloves garlic, chopped
3 tablespoon mixed herbs, chives, parsley, dill, basil
3 tablespoon olive oil

On a baking sheet toss tomatoes, garlic, herbs, and oil, season with salt and pepper and roast in 350 degree oven for 20 minutes. Pack in a lidded plastic container. Make sure to cook these the day of the picnic. Keep warm.

Coffee Almond Brownies

1 cup butter
2 cups sugar
4 eggs
3 tablespoons espresso powder
1 cup flour
1 cup cocoa powder
1/2 teaspoon baking powder
1/2 teaspoon salt
1 teaspoon almond extract
1/2 teaspoon vanilla

Shortcut: Use box brownies if you are in a hurry preparing as on box, but adding 3 tbl instant coffee and 1/4 tsp almond extract.

Preheat oven to 350 and grease a 9x13 baking pan. Melt butter and chocolate together and set aside to cool. In a bowl mix eggs, sugar and espresso powder. Mix in melted chocolate. In a separate bowl mix flour, cocoa powder, baking powder, and salt, stir in chocolate mixture and bake for 30-40 minutes or until a knife inserted in the center comes out clean. Pack in a container.   These can be made the day ahead.

4 plastic bags filled with ½ cup steak cubes and ½ cup cherry or grape tomatoes
4 brownies wrapped in parchment paper
4 juice boxes or bags

Place one wrapped brownie and top with 1 bag of steak and tomatoes, wrap all with twine or jute and tie in a bow. Serve with 1 juice box.

Good quality brats, grilled
Spicy Brown Mustard
Good quality jarred sauerkraut heated
Sliced red onions
4 French bread rolls or German brotchen, if they are available to you

Pack all components in separate containers, keeping brats and sauerkraut warm.

Mustard Bacon Potato Salad

2 lb red new potato
4 strips bacon
For Dressing:
1 tablespoon mustard
1/2 cup red wine vinegar
1 teaspoon honey
1/2 teaspoon salt
1/2 teaspoon pepper
3 tablespoon flat leaf parsley

Cook potatoes in salted boiling water until a knife inserted in center comes out easily. Drain and let cool slightly, cut into quarters. Meanwhile, cook bacon until crisp. Chop and set aside. In hot bacon grease cook quartered potatoes until slightly crispy. In a small bowl combine dressing ingredients and

toss with potatoes. Pack and keep warm until ready to serve. Alternately
this can be served at room temperature or cold.

Apple Strudel

1/2 cup raisins
3 tablespoon dark rum
4 apples cored and sliced
1/4 cup brown sugar
2 teaspoon cinnamon
3 tablespoon flour
2 sheets puff pastry

Preheat oven to 350. In a small bowl combine rum and raisins and set aside
for 30 minutes. In another bowl combine sliced apples, sugar, cinnamon,
flour and macerated raisins with liquid. Lay out both sheets of puff pastry.
Down the center of one spoon half of the mixture. Roll pastry and seal
overlapped edges. Repeat with second sheet. Place on greased cookies
sheet and bake for 35-40 minutes until crust is golden brown. This can be
done the day ahead, but serve at room temperature. Pack in a plastic
container and slice at picnic site. Alternately you can slice at home and pack
in individual container or wrap in fun paper and pack.

Pigs in a Picnic Blanket

1 can crescent rolls
6 hotdogs
Ketchup

Preheat oven to 350. Lay out crescent roll. Roll up hotdogs in squares and place on cookie sheet. Bake for 15-20 minutes or until pastry is golden and crisp. Decorate with ketchup faces.

Dirty Cucumbers

1 seedless cucumber
1/2 teaspoon Hawaiian pink sea salt or kosher salt tinted with food coloring

Cut cucumber in half and then into spears. At picnic site sprinkle with colored salt.

Bug Juice

4 cups sprite
4 scoops lime sherbet
4 dum dum lollypops
1 fruit by the foot

Cut fruit by the foot to look like bugs wings. Roll some of the fruit by the foot into eyes. Decorate dum dum to look like a bug. Pack lime sherbet in your soft sided cooler surrounded by frozen packs.   At picnic site place one scoop of the lime sherbet into a cup add 1 cup of sprite, 1 drop green food coloring, and decorate with dum dum.

Winter

Snowmen fall from heaven, some assembly
required
-Author Unknown

The Hunters Basket

Appetizer: Artichoke Dip
Orange basted Quail
 Chili Butter Filled Roasted Corn
Grilled Zucchini and Mint
Oatmeal, Chocolate Cranberry Cookies
Drink: Guinness Beer
Kids menu: The Runaway Chicken: Mini Quails, grilled zucchini, butter corn and oatmeal chocolate cranberry cookies with chocolate milk (Yohoo)

Mediterranean Taste Basket

Appetizer: Hummus
Lamb and Spicy Sweet Potato Puree in Pita
Garbanzo Bean Salad
Fried Lime and Salt Plantains
Drink: Merlot
Kids menu: A Pocket full of Fun: Ham and cheese pitas, Garbanzo bean salad, Smores, Mix your own Milk

A German Dinner

Appetizer: Tapenade
Cold Cuts, Mixed Cheeses
Pickles & Olives
Baguette
Basil Mayonnaise
Plum Torte
Drink: Mulled Wine
Kids Menu: Hansel and Gretel Sandwiches: Kids make their own sandwiches with the selection of meat and cheese on baguette, plum torte and white grape juice to drink

Italian Basket

Appetizer: Procuitto, Basil, Ricotta Dip
Make your own Pizza
Grilled Olive Polenta
Brownies Iced with Ganache topped with chopped strawberries and basil
Drink: Orange Hot Chocolate
Kids Menu: The Leaning Tower of Pizza Basket, mini pizzas, a mini skewer of cherry tomatoes, olives and cheese, brownies with ganache, and hot chocolate to drink

An English Inspiration

Appetizer: Mustard Bacon Stuffed Cornish Game Hens
Potato Soup
Blueberry Scones
Drink: Hot Buttered Rum
Kids Menu: The London Bridge: A long skewer of cherry tomatoes, buttered potato pieces, pieces of Cornish hen and blueberries, Bobbing for Apples Drink

Artichoke Dip

1 14 oz can artichoke, chopped
1 c mayonnaise
8 oz cream cheese, softened
1 c jack cheese

1/2 c parmesan cheese

1 clove garlic grated
1/2 teaspoon salt
1/2 teaspoon pepper
1/4 teaspoon chipotle pepper
(optional
Pita wedges or crackers

Preheat oven to 350. Mix all ingredients in a heatproof dish. Bake for 15 minutes or until bubbly and golden on top. You can wrap your container in foil and then in a tea towel to keep warm until the picnic. Serve with crackers or pita wedges.

Orange Basted Quail

8 quail or 4 Cornish Hens
1/2 cup good quality orange marmalade
1/4 cup squeezed orange juice
2 teaspoon soy sauce
1/2 teaspoon grated ginger
1/2 teaspoon salt
1/2 teaspoon pepper

Heat grill on high. In a bowl mix orange marmalade, orange juice, soy sauce, ginger, salt and pepper.   Baste quail with orange glaze, salt and pepper on both sides and grill for 3-4 minutes per side basting as you turn the quail over. This can be done at home or at picnic site. If done at home wrap the quail in foil and then in a sealable bag to prevent leaking

Shortcut: Substitute good quality citrus basting sauce for orange marmalade sauce. Use chicken breast instead of quail.

and pack for picnic. Keep warm until ready to serve.   Bring the glaze along and brush quail just before serving.

Chili Butter Roasted Corn

4 ears of corn with husk on
1/2 cup butter, softened
1/2 teaspoon good quality chili powder
1/4 teaspoon salt
1/4 teaspoon pepper

In a small plastic container mix butter, chili powder, salt, pepper, and pack until you reach picnic site. Keep butter cold. Grill corn with husk on until corn is tender and slightly charred about 12-15 minutes. This can be done at home and the corn wrapped in tin foil until ready to eat or grilled at picnic site. Peal back husk, but do not break off. This makes a great handle.
Slather each piece with the chili butter and serve.

Grilled Zucchini and Mint

3 med zucchini, sliced lengthwise
1/4 cup olive oil
1/4 cup mint chopped
1/2 teaspoon salt and pepper

Heat grill on high. Brush each slice of zucchini with olive oil and salt and pepper. Grill on high until soft and golden brown. Remove from heat and top with chopped mint. Keep warm until ready to serve. Serve with extra olive oil for drizzling.

Oatmeal Chocolate Cranberry Cookies

1 c brown sugar
1/2 cup white sugar
1 c butter, softened
1 teaspoon vanilla

2 eggs
1 teaspoon baking soda

1/2 teaspoon baking powder
1/2 teaspoon salt

3 cup quick cooking or old fashioned oats
1 cup flour
1/2 cup cocoa powder
1 cup dried cranberries

Tip: You can add a handful of sliced almonds or dried cherries into the cookies too!

Preheat oven to 350. With a paddle attachment cream together both sugars and butter for 3 minutes. Add eggs, vanilla, and cream for another 3 minutes. In a separate bowl, sift dry ingredients except cranberries. Add dry ingredients to butter mixture and mix until just combined. Add cranberries. Spoon out on cookie sheet and bake for 9-11 minutes. This can be done the day ahead.

4 quail, cooked as above
4 boxes or bottles of Yohoo

Butter Roasted Corn

4 ears of corn with husk on
1/2 cup butter, softened
1/4 teaspoon salt
1/4 teaspoon pepper

In a small plastic container mix butter, salt, pepper, and pack until you reach picnic site. Grill corn with husk on until corn is tender and slightly charred about 12-15 minutes. This can be done at home and the corn wrapped in tin foil until ready to eat or grilled at picnic site. Peal back husk, but do not break off. This makes a great handle. Slather each piece with the chili butter and serve.

Grilled Zucchini and Mint

See recipe above

Oatmeal Chocolate Cranberry Cookies

See Recipe above

Hummus

1 14 oz can garbanzo beans
1/4 c tahini, sesame paste
2 cloves garlic
1/4 c lemon juice
Salt and pepper to taste
6 pita pockets

Place all ingredients in a blender except pita pockets and blend until smooth. Salt and pepper to taste. Pack in a plastic container. This can be done the day ahead. Cut pita pockets into wedges and pack in a plastic bag.   At picnic site serve hummus surrounded by pita wedges.

Lamb and Spicy Sweet Potato Puree in Pita

2 lamb shoulder chops
2 sweet potatoes
2 teaspoon chipotle in adobe sauce
1/4 cup butter

Shortcut: If you are short on time, pick up good quality hummus from your local grocery store on the way to the picnic

Tip: The sweet potatoes can be cooked in the microwave until soft.

1/2 teaspoon salt
1/4 teaspoon pepper
2 c spinach
4 pita pockets

Heat grill on high heat. Salt and pepper both sides of lamb and grill until medium rare or a thermometer reads 145 degrees. Lamb can be grilled at the picnic site or at home. If grilled at home wrap in tin foil and a sealable bag and keep warm until picnic. Peal, chop and steam sweet potatoes. Mash sweet potatoes, chipotle, butter, salt and pepper. Pack in a plastic container. Pack spinach and pita pockets. At picnic site, slice lamb against the grain, cut pitas in half and fill with 3-4 tablespoons spicy sweet potato puree, a few leaves of spinach and a few pieces of lamb.

Garbanzo Bean Salad

1 14 oz can garbanzo beans
2 small cans sliced black olives
1/4 cup cilantro chopped
1/4 cup red wine vinegar
2 teaspoon cumin, ground

Drain garbanzo beans and olives. Mix all ingredients in a plastic container. Alternately, you can pack individual salads in small pickling jars or small plastic containers.

Fried Lime and Salt Plantains

2 plantains
1/4 cup oil
Zest of 2 limes
2 teaspoon kosher salt

Slice plantains into 1/2 inch pieces. Heat oil on medium high and fry plantains until golden brown on both sides. Allow to cool. Use the bottom of a glass and mash plantains flat. Refry until crisp, 2-3 minutes per side. Top with lime zest, juice and salt. Pack in a paper bag. Bring extra lime and salt for guests to top their plantains.

Figs in Honey

12 fresh figs
1/4 cup honey

Pack figs and honey. At picnic site, slice figs into quarters but not cutting all the way through. Your are essentially making the fig look like a flower. Drizzle with honey. Serve 3 figs per plate and enjoy!

Ham and Cheese Pita

2 Pitas cut in half to make 4 pitas
1 cup of Ham cubes
1 cup of shredded cheese
4 Cherry Tomatoes

Fill each pita half with ¼ cup of ham
and ¼ cup of shredded cheese. Slice
each cherry tomato into 4 wedges
and top each pita sandwich with 4
wedges of tomato (1 whole tomato).
Wrap sandwich in a piece of wax
paper or parchment paper and tie
with a long strip of material or a
ribbon and place into a container or
plastic bag to transport.

Garbanzo Bean Salad

See recipe above

Mix Your Own Milk

4 cups of milk (bring extra for seconds)
4 small whisks
Various milk flavors, chocolate, strawberry, malt, ect.
4 large fun plastic cups
4 fun straws

Pack a small container of milk in a zip lock and surround it with crushed ice.
Buy 4 small whisks at your local dollar store and give each child a cup of milk

and a whisk. Add their choice of milk flavoring and let each child whip up their creation! Depending on how your flavors come packaged-you may want to repackage them in Ziplocs with plastics spoons in each bag for easy transporting and serving.

S'mores
You will need to build a fire for this one-so you will have to look for a location that allows fires.

16 squares of graham crackers (bring a couple extra in case some break)
8 large marshmallows
8 squares of chocolate
8 long sticks to use to roast marshmallows

Place 8 graham cracker squares on a plate and place the chocolate squares on top. Roast 8 marshmallows and place the roasted marshmallow on the graham cracker squares with chocolate. Top with the remaining 8 graham cracker squares and squish down! Enjoy!

Tapenade

1 jar green olives drained
1/4 cup flat leaf parsley
2 cloves garlic
2 tablespoon capers
3 tablespoon lemon juice
1/2 cup olive oil
Salt and pepper to taste

Combine all ingredients in a food processor and process until smooth. This can be made the day ahead.

Basil Mayonnaise

1 cup mayonnaise
1/4 cup chopped basil
1 clove garlic, grated
1/4 teaspoon pepper

Mix all ingredients and pack in a small plastic container. Keep cool-put in plastic bag and place ice around the container.

Serve tapenade, cold cuts, mixed cheeses, pickles, olives, condiments and bread on a large platter family style.

Tip: Try a different herb for your next picnic!

Plum Torte

1 sheet puff pastry
1 lb plums
4 oz cream cheese,
softened
1/4 c sugar
1 egg
3 tablespoons plum
jelly, apple can be
substituted
1/4 teaspoon
cinnamon

Preheat oven to
375. Pit plums and
thinly slice. In a
bowl, whisk the

Tip: Try a different fruit if plums are not in season in your area!

cream cheese, sugar, and eggs. Lay out puff pastry on a cookie sheet. With a sharp knife cut a 1/2 inch border around the puff pastry without cutting all the way through. When the pastry cooks it will puff outside of where you cut. Spread the cream cheese mixture on the pastry sheet up to where you cut the boarder. Arrange plums on top of cream cheese and brush with plum jam. Sprinkle with cinnamon. Also, brush the edges of the puff pastry with the jam. Bake for 20-30 minutes until cream cheese is set and puff pastry is golden. If the pastry becomes brown before the cheese is set lightly cover with tin foil.   Let cool.   Pack in a plastic container with a lid.

Mulled Wine

1 bottle red wine
1/2 teaspoon cinnamon or 4 cinnamon sticks
4 cloves
1 pinch nutmeg
1/2 cup sugar
3/4 cup amaretto

Mix all ingredients in a saucepan. Heat until just below a boil. Pack in a thermos.

Hansel and Gretel Sandwiches

4 baguettes, sliced open
4 slices of meat
4 slices of cheese
Various condiments
Tomato and cucumber slices
Give the children a baguette and let them pick their own meat and cheese.
Top with their choice of condiment and tomato or cucumber slices.

Grape Juice

4 cups of white grape juice
16 frozen white grapes
4 large fun plastic cups
4 fun straws
Freeze your grapes (16 grapes) the night before in a small zip lock and then put them in your cooler bag the next morning just before leaving for the picnic.
Fill each cup with grape juice and add 4 frozen grapes to each cup. Add a fun straw and enjoy!

Prosciutto, Basil, and Ricotta dip
1 12 oz ricotta
1/2 cup basil chopped
1/4 lb prosciutto, chopped
1 lemon
1 clove garlic, grated
1-pint grape tomatoes

In a bowl, combine ricotta, basil, prosciutto, the juice of ½ a lemon and garlic. If possible, make this the night before, as it gets better when the flavors have time to meld. Keep cool until ready to serve. Serve with grape tomatoes.

Make Your Own Pizza
For the crust:
1 package active dry yeast
1 teaspoon honey
1 cup warm water
1 tablespoon kosher salt
Extra-virgin olive oil
3 cups flour
For the toppings:
Tomato sauce
Goat cheese
Roasted Garlic

Pesto
Cooked sausage
Bacon
Prosciutto
Sliced red onion
Sliced peppers
Chopped wild mushrooms
Olives, black and green
Parmesan cheese
Mozzarella cheese

Shortcut: Use good quality prepared crusts or defrosted bread dough.

For the dough: In the bowl of a standing electric mixer fitted with a dough hook, combine the yeast, honey, and warm water; stir gently to dissolve. Let the mixture stand about 5 to 10 minutes. Mix in the salt and 3 tablespoons of olive oil. Add the flour, a little at a time, mixing at the lowest speed until all the flour has been incorporated. Increase the speed to medium until dough has come together about 5 minutes. Place dough in an oiled bowl and let rise until doubled, about 1 hour. Punch down the dough and divide into 4 balls. Pat out balls into individual sized pizza's and drizzle with olive oil on both sides. If you are grilling at the picnic site place pizza dough's sprinkled with corn meal between sheets of parchment paper and into a zip bag for transport. Grill dough on a medium high 4-5 minutes per side. At that point your guests can choose their toppings and top their pizza. Place in the grill for a few more minutes to melt cheese and warm toppings.

Grilled Olive Polenta

1 cup cornmeal
2 cup water
1 cup chopped olives
1/2 cup parmesan cheese
1/4 cup olive oil

In a saucepan, bring water to a boil. Add cornmeal while whisking at the same time. Remove from heat and stir in chopped olives and cheese. Turn hot polenta onto a counter, pat into a square, and let cool. When cooled cut into wedges or squares. At this point, you can pack the polenta and olive oil and grill at the picnic site. Brush polenta with olive oil and grill over high heat until the outside is golden and crispy.

Brownies iced with Ganache topped with chopped strawberries and basil

1 cup butter
2 cups sugar
4 eggs
1 cup flour
1 cup cocoa powder
1/2 teaspoon baking powder
1/2 teaspoon salt
1 teaspoon almond extract
1/2 teaspoon vanilla

Ganache
1/2 cup cream
1 cup chocolate pieces or chunks
Strawberries
1 basket of strawberries
1/4 cup chopped basil

Preheat oven to 350 and grease a 9x13 baking pan. Melt the butter, stir in sugar and eggs. In separate bowl mix flour, cocoa powder, baking powder, and salt. Combine dry mixture to wet mixture. Bake for 30 minutes. Or until a knife inserted in the center comes out clean. For the ganache warm cream, drop in chocolate, when melted stir to combine. At picnic site top brownies with ganache, chopped strawberries and chopped basil.

Orange Hot Chocolate

4 c milk
6 oz dark chocolate, chopped
1 c Grand Marnier (Orange Liquor)

Bring milk to a boil, add chocolate and remove from heat. Whisk until all chocolate has melted. Stir in Grand Marnier. Pack in a thermos. Do not forget to pack the mugs to serve-enjoy!

Make Your Own Pizza

For the crust: Use small tortillas or pre-made small pizza crusts

For the toppings:
Tomato sauce
Cooked sausage
Bacon
Prosciutto
Sliced red onion
Sliced peppers
Olives, black and green
Parmesan cheese
Mozzarella cheese
Roasted Garlic

Tip: You can also make small pizza crusts from the dough that you make for the adult menu.

Give each child a plate with a tortilla on it and let them add which toppings they like. An adult should place the pizza on the grill and grill until warm and cheese is melted. Use kitchen scissors to cut into wedges, serve and enjoy!

Mini Leaning Tower

8 toothpicks-2 skewers per child
8 cherry tomatoes
8 olives
8 cubes of cheese

For each toothpick, add 1 olive, 1 cube of cheese and 1 cherry tomato. Serve 2 skewers per child-Enjoy. Assemble all skewers at home and place in a zip lock to transport to your site. Alternatively, wrap by twos and place in your container, if your are serving individual bags.

Brownies iced with Gnache topped with Strawberries

See recipe above and omit basil

Orange Hot Chocolate

4 c milk
6 oz dark chocolate, chopped
Orange Zest
Bring milk to a boil, add chocolate and remove from heat. Whisk until all chocolate has melted. Pack in a thermos. At the picnic site pour hot chocolate into mugs and zest orange over mug. Slice the orange into wedges after you have put orange zest on all the mugs and serve a mug of orange hot chocolate and 2 orange wedges.

Dried Apricots and Ham

1/4 pound Turkish apricots
1/4 pound Good quality honey ham

Serve apricots next to rolled up ham pieces.

Stuffed Cornish Game Hens

4 small Cornish game hens
2 pieces bacon, uncooked
1 stick butter
2 tablespoon mustard
1/4 teaspoon salt
1/2teaspoon pepper

In a food processor, combine bacon, butter, mustard, salt and pepper. Push on hens to break the bones in the cavity so that the hen is as flat as you can get it. Loosen skin on breast side of hens and legs and stuff with the bacon mixture.   Salt and pepper outside of hens. At this point, you can pack the hens and grill them at the picnic site or grill them at home. Heat grill on med high. Place hens on grill and weight

down with bricks covered in tin foil. Cook hens 8 minutes on each side. Do not flip them more than once or the skin will stick. Keep warm until ready to serve.

Potato Soup

3 cloves garlic, chopped
1 leak, cleaned and sliced
2 tablespoon olive oil
1 baking potatoes, pealed and chopped
1 cup white wine
4 c stock, chicken or vegetable
1/2 cup cream
1/4 cup chives, chopped
Salt and pepper

Heat oil in stockpot on medium high. Add leaks and garlic and cook until soft. Add potatoes and cook for 2-3 minutes. Add wine and stock and bring to simmer and cook until potatoes are tender. Either in a blender or with an immersion blender blend soup until creamy. Add cream and salt and pepper to taste. This can be done the day ahead and then reheated just before leaving.   Pack in a thermos. At picnic site, ladle soup into bowls or cups and drizzle with cream and chives.

Blueberry Scones

2 cup flour
3 teaspoon baking powder
1 teaspoon baking soda
1/2 teaspoon salt
1/2 cup sugar
1 stick butter, cold
1 c cream + 2 Tablespoons
1 cup dried blueberries

Preheat oven to 350. In a large bowl, combine flour, baking powder, baking soda, salt, and sugar. Cut in butter. Toss in blueberries. Make a well in the center and add cream. Mix working from the outside in with your hands being careful not to crush the blueberries. When almost combined, turn out and push together once or twice. Pat into a 12 inch square and cut into wedges. Place on a cookie sheet and brush with remaining cream and sprinkle with sugar. Bake for 15-20 minutes until golden brown.

Hot Buttered Rum

2 cups dark brown sugar
1/2 cup butter, softened
1 cup vanilla ice cream, melted
1 teaspoon cinnamon
8 oz rum
4 cinnamon sticks

Beat sugar, butter, ice cream and cinnamon until combined. Pack in a lidded plastic container and store in freezer. This can be done up to a week in advance. Pack butter batter in a cooler bag. Pack boiling water in a thermos. Pack rum separately. At the picnic site scoop 1/2 cup batter into a mug. Top with 2 oz rum and water to fill the mug. Serve with a cinnamon stick for stirring.

The London Bridge

4 Long skewers
4 large strawberries
8 blueberries
8 cherry tomatoes
8 potato pieces, cooked with butter and salt
8 pieces of cooked Cornish hen

For each skewer, place the 2 blueberries and strawberry at the end. Then alternate the pieces tomatoes, potatoes and Cornish hen pieces. End the skewer with a tomato to hold the food in place. Roll each skewer in a piece of parchment paper and tie with a piece of twine. Stamp each child's first initial on a piece of paper and attach it to the skewer with the twine. Place all skewers in a large zip lock to transport to the site.

Buttered Potatoes

3 cloves garlic, chopped
2 leaks, cleaned and sliced
2 tablespoon olive oil
2 baking potatoes, pealed and chopped
1/4 cup chives, chopped
Salt and pepper

Heat oil in stockpot on medium high. Add leaks and garlic and cook until soft. Add potatoes and cook for 2-3 minutes. Add salt and pepper to taste and stir in chives.

Stuffed Cornish Game Hens

See recipe above

Shortcut: Use a store bought rotisserie chicken instead of the Cornish hens

Bobbing for Apples Drink

4 cups of apple juice
4 toothpicks
4 large plastic fun cups
4 fun straws
1 apple, cubed

For each toothpick, add 4 pieces of the cubed apple. Place all toothpicks in a zip lock to transport to the site. At the site, fill each glass with 1 cup of apple juice and drop in 1 toothpick with apples and add a fun straw and enjoy!

CPSIA information can be obtained at www.ICGtesting.com
Printed in the USA
BVIW12n1824031016
464025BV00013B/88